Practical
Spirituality

Reflections on the Spiritual Basis
of Nonviolent Communication

A Nonviolent Communication™
presentation and workshop transcription by

Marshall B. Rosenberg, PhD

PuddleDancer
P R E S S

P.O. Box 231129, Encinitas, CA 92023-1129
email@PuddleDancer.com • www.PuddleDancer.com

For additional information:
Center for Nonviolent Communication
9301 Indian School Rd., NE, Suite 204, Albuquerque, NM 87112
Ph: 505-244-4041 • Fax: 505-247-0414 • Email: cnvc@cnvc.org • Website: www.cnvc.org

Practical Spirituality
Reflections on the Spiritual Basis of Nonviolent Communication

PuddleDancer Press, Permissions Dept.
2240 Encinitas Blvd., Ste. D-911, Encinitas, CA 92024
Tel: 1-760-652-5754 Fax: 1-760-274-6400
www.NonviolentCommunication.com Email@PuddleDancer.com

Ordering Information:
Please contact Independent Publishers Group, Tel: 312-337-0747;
Fax: 312-337-5985; Email: frontdesk@ipgbook.com or visit
www.IPGbook.com for other contact information and details
about ordering online

Author: Marshall B. Rosenberg, PhD
Editor: Graham Van Dixhorn, Write to Your Market, Inc.,
        www.writetoyourmarket.com
Cover and Interior Design: Lightbourne, Inc.,
        www.lightbourne.com
Cover photograph: www.gettyimages.com

Manufactured in the United States of America

1st Printing, October 2005

10 9 8 7 6 5

ISBN: 978-1-892005-14-4

Contents

Q: How do we connect with the Divine through
Nonviolent Communication? 2

Q: What does "God" mean to you? 2

Q: What is your favorite way of knowing Beloved
Divine Energy? 3

Q: What religious beliefs, teachings, or writings
have had the greatest influence on you? 3

Q: Doesn't the influence of religion and spirituality
promote passivity, or an "opiate of the masses"
effect? 4

Q: So Nonviolent Communication evolved in part
from spiritual origins? 5

Q: What do you mean by "giving of ourselves"? 6

Q: Nonviolent Communication came out of your
desire to manifest love? 7

Q: How do you prevent Ego from interfering
with your connection with God? 8

Q: Then you believe that the language of our culture
prevents us from knowing our Divine Energy
more intimately? 9

Q: Is this the spiritual basis of Nonviolent
Communication? 10

Q: Is this lack of connection to Divine Energy
responsible for violence in the world? 10

Q: How do we overcome this conditioning? 12

Q: We gain this connection to each other by
knowing God? 13

Q: So exactly how do we gain this connection to
Divine Energy, and to other people? 14

Q: How do we express what's alive in us? 14

Q: Do you suggest that simply telling people how
we feel is all that's needed? 16

Q: What prevents people from just saying what
they need? 17

Q: So what's next after feelings and needs? 18

Q: What keeps us from connecting to the life in
each other as you suggest? 19

Q: Can you give an example of how to make an
empathic connection with someone? 20

Q: How do you express your needs as requests
without sounding like you're demanding
something? 22

Q: What about discipline? What you're suggesting
sounds like just being permissive. 23

Q: How can I tell when I'm connecting to what's
alive in someone else? 25

Q: Can you give another example of how you've
actually used this process to connect with others? ... 25

Q: The process of connecting to the Divine Energy
in others with NVC seems clear enough on paper,
but isn't it hard to actually live by? 27

Q: How do you get enemies to recognize the Divine
   in each other? 28

Q: How basic is our need to give to one another? 29

Q: Have you encountered any cultural or language
   barriers to this process? 30

Q: Do you believe a spiritual practice is important
   for practicing nonviolence? 31

Q: Have you been influenced by past movements
   that have attempted to mediate between
   spirituality and social change, like Gandhi's or
   Martin Luther King Jr.'s? 32

The Four-Part Nonviolent Communication Process 33

Some Basic Feelings and Needs We All Have 34

About PuddleDancer Press 35

About the Center for Nonviolent Communication 36

Trade Books From PuddleDancer Press 37

Trade Booklets From PuddleDancer Press 41

About the Author 42

Practical
Spirituality

A Q&A Session with
Marshall B. Rosenberg, PhD

Whenever Marshall Rosenberg speaks about deeply held beliefs—spirituality, concepts of God, views of love—two themes always emerge: 1) the greatest joy springs from connecting to life by contributing to our own and others' well-being, and 2) spirituality and love are more about what we do than what we feel.

People frequently ask Marshall how he got to that place, how he relates to the religious beliefs of others, and what his views mean for the practice of Nonviolent Communication. What follows are excerpts of Marshall's unscripted, verbal responses to queries from media interviewers and workshop participants on the subject of spirituality, the concept of the Divine, the spiritual basis of NVC, and applying NVC values to social change.

Q: How do we connect with the Divine through Nonviolent Communication?

A: I think it is important that people see that spirituality is at the base of Nonviolent Communication, and that they learn the mechanics of the NVC process with that in mind. It's really a spiritual practice that I am trying to show as a way of life. Even though we don't make a point of mentioning this, people get seduced by the practice. Even if they practice NVC as a mechanical technique, they start to experience things between themselves and other people they weren't able to experience before. So eventually they come to the spirituality of the process. They begin to see that it's more than a communication process and realize it's really an attempt to manifest our spirituality. I have tried to integrate the spirituality into the practice of NVC in a way that meets my need not to destroy the beauty of it through abstract philosophizing.

The kind of world I'd like to live in will require some rather significant social changes, but the changes that I'd like to see happen probably won't happen unless the people working toward them are coming out of a different spirituality than what has led to the predicaments we're in now. So, our training is designed to help people make sure that the spirituality that's guiding them is one of their own choosing and not one they've internalized by the culture. And that they proceed in creating social change out of that spirituality.

Q: What does "God" mean to you?

A: I need a way to think of God that works for me—other words or ways to look at this beauty, this powerful energy—and so my name for God is "Beloved Divine Energy." For a while it was just Divine Energy but then I was reading some of the Eastern religions, and Eastern poets, and I loved how they had this personal, loving connection with this Energy. And I found that it added to my life to call it Beloved Divine Energy. To me this Beloved Divine Energy is Life, connection to life.

Q: What is your favorite way of knowing Beloved Divine Energy?

A: It is how I connect with human beings. I know Beloved Divine Energy by connecting with human beings in a certain way. I not only see Divine Energy, I taste Divine Energy, I feel Divine Energy, and I am Divine Energy. I'm connected with Beloved Divine Energy when I connect with human beings in this way. Then God is very alive for me.

Q: What religious beliefs, teachings, or writings have had the greatest influence on you?

A: It's hard for me to say which of the various religions on the planet have had the most impact on me. Probably Buddhism as much as any. I like so much of what I understand the Buddha or the people who quoted the Buddha to be saying. For example, the Buddha makes it very clear: Don't get addicted to your strategies, your requests, or your desires. That's a very important part of our training: to not mix real human needs with the way we've been educated to get those needs met. So, be careful to not get your strategies mixed up with your needs. We don't need a new car, for example. Some people may choose a new car as a strategy for meeting a need for reliability or peace of mind, but you've got to watch out, because society can trick you into thinking it's the new car that you really need. This part of our training is very much in harmony with my understanding of the Buddha.

Almost all of the religions and mythologies I've studied say a very similar message, one that Joseph Campbell, the mythologist, summarizes in some of his work: *Don't do anything that isn't play.* And what they mean by play is willingly contributing to life. So, don't do anything to avoid punishment; don't do anything for rewards; don't do anything out of guilt, shame, and the vicious concepts of duty and obligation. What you do will be play when you can see how it enriches life. I get that message from my understanding not only of the Buddha, but also from what I have learned about Islam, Christianity, and Judaism. I think it's a natural language. Do that which contributes to life.

Q: Doesn't the influence of religion and spirituality promote passivity, or an "opiate of the masses" effect?

A: I'm very worried about any spirituality that allows us to just sit comfortably in the world and say, "But I am helping the world, the energy alone coming from me is going to create social change." Rather, I trust a spirituality that leads people to go forward and transform the world, that doesn't just sit there with this beautiful image of radiating energy. I want to see that energy reflected in the person's actions as they go out and make things happen. It's something you do, a practical spirituality.

Q: So Nonviolent Communication evolved in part from spiritual origins?

A: Nonviolent Communication evolved from my attempt to get conscious about Beloved Divine Energy and how to connect with it. I was dissatisfied with input from my chosen field of clinical psychology because it was and is pathology-based and I didn't like its language. It didn't give me a view of the beauty of human beings. So, after I got my degree I decided to go more in the direction of Carl Rogers and Abraham Maslow.

I decided to ask myself the scary questions, "What are we and what are we meant to be?" I found that there was very little written about this in psychology. So I took a crash course in comparative religion because I saw they dealt more with this question. And this word *love* kept coming up in each of them.

I used to hear the word *love* as many people used it—in a religious sense, like, "You should love everybody." I used to get really annoyed at the word *love*. "Oh yeah, I'm supposed to love Hitler?" I didn't know the words *New Age Bullshit*, but I used what was my equivalent then. I tried to understand better what love means because I could see it had so much meaning for so many millions of people in all of these religions. What is it, and how do you "do" this "love"?

Nonviolent Communication really came out of my attempt to understand this concept of love and how to manifest it, how to do it. I came to the conclusion that it was not just something you feel, but it is something we manifest, something we do, something we have. And what is this manifestation? It is giving of ourselves in a certain way.

Q: What do you mean by "giving of ourselves"?

A: To me, giving of ourselves means an honest expression of what's alive in us in this moment. It intrigues me that every culture asks upon greeting each other, "How are you?" They don't use those words. In English they say it this way: *How are you?* In Spanish, *¿Cómo estás?* French is *Comment allez-vous?* German is *Wie Geht es Dir?* We say it as a social ritual, but it's a very important question, because if we're to live in peace and harmony, if we're to enjoy contributing to one another's well-being, we need to know what's alive in one another. It's such an important question. What a gift it is to be able to know at any given moment what is alive in someone.

To give a gift of one's self is a manifestation of love. It's a gift when you reveal yourself nakedly and honestly, at any given moment, for no other purpose than to reveal what's alive in you. Not to blame, criticize, or punish. Just "Here I am, and here is what I would like." This is my vulnerability at this moment. To me, that is a way of manifesting love.

And the other way we give of ourselves is through how we receive another person's message. To receive it empathically, connecting with what's alive in them, making no judgment. Just to hear what is alive in the other person and what they would like. So Nonviolent Communication is just a manifestation of what I understand love to be. In that way it's similar to the Judeo-Christian concepts of "Love your neighbor as yourself" and "Judge not lest you be judged."

Q: Nonviolent Communication came out of your desire to manifest love?

A: I was also helped by empirical research in psychology that defined the characteristics of healthy relationships, and by studying people who were living manifestations of loving people. Out of these sources I pulled together a process that helped me to connect with people in what I could understand is a loving way.

And then I saw what happened when I did connect with people in this way. This beauty, this power connected me with an energy that I choose to call Beloved Divine Energy. So Nonviolent Communication helps me stay connected with that beautiful Divine Energy within myself and to connect with it in others. And certainly when I connect that Divine Energy within myself with the Divine Energy in others, what happens is the closest thing to knowing what it is to be connected to God.

It helps to remember that a key purpose of Nonviolent Communication is to connect with other people—and thus with Divine Energy—in a way that enables compassionate giving to take place. It's giving that comes from the heart willingly, where we are giving service to ourselves and others, not out of duty, obligation, not out of fear of punishment, hope for a reward, not out of guilt or shame, but for what I consider is our nature, our nature to enjoy giving to one another. In Nonviolent Communication, we strive to connect with one another in a way that allows our nature to come forward. When I say that I think it's our nature to enjoy giving, some people may wonder whether I'm a little bit naïve and unaware of all the violence in the world. How can I think it's our nature to enjoy compassionate giving with what's happening in the world? Unfortunately, I see the violence. I work in places like Rwanda, Israel, Palestine, Sri Lanka, and I'm well aware of all the violence in the world, but I don't think that's our nature.

In every place that I work I ask people the following: "Think of something you've done within the last twenty-four hours that in some way has contributed to making life more wonderful for somebody." And when they've recalled something I then say, "Now, how do you feel when you are aware of how that act contributed to making life more wonderful for somebody?" And everybody has a smile on their face. You see, when we are aware of the power we have to enrich life, it feels good: It feels good to serve life. And then I ask people, "Can anybody think of anything that's more fulfilling in life than to use our efforts this way?" And I've asked that question all over our planet and everyone seems in agreement. There's nothing that is better, nothing that feels better, nothing is more enjoyable than using our efforts in the service of life, contributing to one another's well-being.

Q: *How do you prevent Ego from interfering with your connection with God?*

A: By seeing Ego as very closely tied to the way my culture has trained me to think, and trained me to communicate. And how the culture has trained me to meet my needs in certain ways, to get my needs mixed up with strategies I might use to meet my needs. So I try to remain conscious of these three ways that the culture has programmed me to do things that really aren't in my best interest, to function more from Ego than from my connection with Divine Energy. I have tried to learn ways for training myself to become conscious of this culturally learned thinking, and I've incorporated these into Nonviolent Communication.

Q: Then you believe that the language of our culture prevents us from knowing our Divine Energy more intimately?

A: Oh yes, definitely. I think our language makes it really hard, especially the language given to us by the cultural training most of us seem to have gone through, and the associations the word *God* brings up for many people. Judgmental, or right/wrong thinking, is one of the hardest things I've found to overcome in teaching Nonviolent Communication over the years. The people that I work with have all gone to schools and churches and, if they like Nonviolent Communication, it's very easy for them to say it's the "right way" to communicate. It's very easy to think that Nonviolent Communication is the goal.

I've altered a Buddhist parable that relates to this question. Imagine a beautiful, whole, and sacred place. And imagine that you could really know God when you are in that place. But let's say that there is a river between you and that place and you'd like to get to that place, but you've got to get over this river to do it. So you get a raft, and this raft is a real handy tool to get you across the river. Once you're across the river, you can walk the rest of the several miles to this beautiful place. But the Buddhist parable ends by saying that, "One is a fool who continues on to the sacred place carrying the raft on their back."

Nonviolent Communication is a tool to get me ~~~
cultural training so I can get to the place. NVC i
place. If we get addicted to the raft, attached to tl

makes it harder to get to the place. People just learning the process of Nonviolent Communication sometimes forget all about the place. If they get too locked into the raft, the process becomes mechanical.

Nonviolent Communication is one of the most powerful tools that I've found for connecting with people in a way that helps us get connected to the Divine, where what we do toward one another comes out of Divine Energy. That's the place I want to get to.

Q: Is this the spiritual basis of Nonviolent Communication?

A: The spiritual basis for me is that I'm trying to connect with the Divine Energy in others and connect them with the Divine in me, because I believe that when we are really connected with that Divinity within one another and ourselves, that people enjoy contributing to one another's well-being more than anything else. So for me, if we're connected with the Divine in others and ourselves, we are going to enjoy what happens, and that's the spiritual basis. In this place, violence is impossible.

Q: Is this lack of connection to Divine Energy responsible for violence in the world?

A: I would say it this way: I think we have been given the gift of choice to create the world of our choosing. And we've been given this great and abundant world for creating a world of joy and nurturing. To me, violence in the world comes about when we get alienated or disconnected from this Energy.

How do we get connected when we are educated to be disconnected? I believe it's our cultural conditioning and education that disconnects us from God, especially our education *about* God, and I believe that *violence comes because of how we were educated, not because of our nature.* We have been educated, according to the theologian Walter Wink, for about eight thousand years in a way that makes violence enjoyable, that gets us disconnected from our compassionate nature. And why were we educated this way? That's a long story, and I won't go into it here except to say that it started with myths that began to develop long ago about human nature, myths that humans were basically evil, selfish, and that the good life is all about heroic forces crushing evil forces. Wink writes about how domination cultures use certain teachings about God to maintain oppression. That's why priests and kings have often been closely related. The kings needed the priests to justify the oppression, to interpret the holy books in ways that justified punishment, domination, and so forth.

So, we've been living under a destructive mythology for a long time and that destructive mythology requires a certain language. It requires a language that dehumanizes people, turns them into objects. So we have learned to think in terms of moralistic judgments of one another. We have words in our consciousness like right, wrong, good, bad, selfish, unselfish, terrorists, freedom fighters. And connected to these is the concept of justice based on *deserve*, that if you do one of these bad things you deserve to be punished. If you do the good things then you deserve to be rewarded. Unfortunately, for about eight thousand years we have been subjected to that consciousness. I think that's the core of violence on our planet: faulty education. The process of Nonviolent

Communication is an integration of thought, language, and communication that I think brings us closer to our nature. It helps us to connect with one another so that we come back to what is really the fun way to live, which is contributing to one another's well-being.

Q: *How do we overcome this conditioning?*

A: I'm often in between people in a lot of pain. I remember working with twenty Serbians and twenty Croatians. Some of the people there had family members killed by the other side and they all had generations of poison pumped into their heads about the other side. They spent three days expressing their rage and pain to one another. Fortunately, we were there for seven days.

One word I haven't used yet in speaking about the power of NVC is the word *inevitability.* So many times I have seen that no matter what has happened, if people connect in this certain way it is inevitable that they will end up enjoying giving to one another. It is *inevitable.* For me my work is like watching the magic show. It's too beautiful for words.

But sometimes this Divine Energy doesn't work as fast as I think it should. I remember sitting there in the middle of all this rage and pain and thinking, "Divine Energy, if you can heal all this stuff why are you taking so long, why are you putting these people through this?" And the Energy spoke to me, and it said: "You just do what you can to connect. Bring your energy in. Connect and help the other people connect and let me take care of the rest." But even though that was going on in one part of my brain, I knew joy was inevitable if we could just keep getting connected to our own and one another's Divine Energy.

And it happened. It happened with great beauty. The last day everybody was talking about joy. And many of them said, "You know I thought I was never going to feel joy again after what we've been through." This was the theme on everybody's lips. So that evening the twenty Serbians and twenty Croatians, who seven days earlier had only unimaginable pain in relation to one another, danced one another's dances, sang one another's songs, and celebrated the joy of life together.

Q: We gain this connection to each other by knowing God?

A: I want to stay away from intellectualizing about God. If by "knowing God" we mean this intimate connection with Beloved Divine Energy, then we gain every second as experiencing heaven.

The heaven I gain from knowing God is this inevitability, to know it is inevitable that, no matter what the hell is going on if we get to this level of connection with one another, if we get in touch with one another's Divine Energy, it's inevitable that we will enjoy giving and we'll give back to life. I've been through such ugly stuff with people that I don't get worried about it anymore. It's inevitable. If we get that quality of connection, we'll like where it gets us.

It amazes me how effective it is. I could tell you similar examples between the extremist Israelis, both politically and religiously, and the same on the Palestinian side, and between the Hutus and the Tutsis, and Christian and Muslim tribes in Nigeria. With all of them it amazes me how easy it is to bring about this reconciliation and healing.

Once again, all we have to do is get both sides connected to the other person's needs. To me the needs are the quickest, closest way to getting in connection with that Divine Energy. Everyone has the same needs. The needs come because we're alive.

Q: So exactly how do we gain this connection to Divine Energy, and to other people?

A: There are two basic parts to the process. The first is learning how to express ourselves in a language of life. The other half of the process is how we respond to other people's messages. In Nonviolent Communication, we try to keep our attention focused by answering two critical questions: *What's alive in us?* and *What can we do to make life more wonderful?*

The first question, "What's alive in me; what's alive in you?" is a question that all over the planet people ask themselves when they get together: How are you?

Sadly, though most people ask the question, very few people really know how to answer it very well because we haven't been educated in a language of life. We've not really been taught to answer the question. We ask it, yes, but we don't know how to answer it. Nonviolent Communication, as we'll see, suggests how we can let people know what's alive in us. It shows us how to connect with what's alive in other people, even if they don't have words for saying it.

Q: How do we express what's alive in us?

A: Expressing what's alive in us requires literacy on three levels.

First of all, it requires being able to answer the question "What's alive in you?" without mixing in any evaluation. That's what I call an **observation**. *What do people do* that we either like or don't like? That's important information to communicate. To tell people what's alive in us, we need to tell the other person what they're doing that is supporting life in us, *and* what they're doing that isn't supporting life in us. But it's very important to learn how to say that to people without mixing in any evaluation. So, this is the first step in trying to tell people what's alive in us: to be able to call their attention—concretely, specifically—to what the person's doing that we like or don't like and not mix in any evaluation.

With an observation in mind of what this person does, if we're to use Nonviolent Communication we want to be honest with them about it. But honesty of a different kind than telling people what's wrong with them. Honesty from the heart, not honesty that implies wrongness. We want to go inside and tell the person what's alive in us when this person does this. And this involves the other two forms of literacy we need: feeling literacy and need literacy. *To say clearly what's alive in us at any given moment we have to be clear about what we feel and what we need.* So, let's start with the feelings.

We have **feelings** every moment. The problem is that we haven't learned how to be conscious of what's alive in us. Our consciousness has been more directed to make us look outward to what authority thinks we are. There are different ways we might express our feelings depending on what culture we grow up in, but it is important to have a vocabulary of feelings that really does just describe what's alive in us that doesn't include interpretations of other people. We don't want to use words like *misunderstood*, because that's not really a feeling, that's more how we are analyzing whether the other person has understood us or not. If we think somebody has misunderstood us sometimes we can be angry, frustrated, it could be many different things. Likewise, we don't want to use words like *manipulated*, or *criticized*. They're not what we call feelings in our training. Sadly, very few people have much of a feeling vocabulary and I see the cost of that very often in my work.

Is it really an expression of what's alive in you, your feelings? Make sure that it's not a thought-diagnosis of others. Go into your heart. How do you feel when the other person does what they do?

(Editor's note: for complete feelings and needs vocabularies, please see *Nonviolent Communication: A Language of Life* by Marshall B. Rosenberg, PhD)

Q: *Do you suggest that simply telling people how we feel is all that's needed?*

A: No, feelings can be used in a destructive way if we try to imply that other people's behavior is the cause of our feelings. *The cause of our feelings is our needs, not other people's behavior.* And this is the third component of expressing what's alive in us: **needs**. Getting connected to what's alive in us is getting connected to our own Divine Energy.

In my neighborhood when I was six years old, we used to say this when somebody would call us a name: "Sticks and stones can break my bones, but names could never hurt me." We were aware then that it's *not what other people do that can hurt you; it's how you take it*. But, we were educated in guilt-inducing ways by authorities, teachers, parents, who used guilt to mobilize us to do what they wanted. They would express feelings this way, "It hurts me when you don't clean up your room." "You make me angry when you hit your brother." We've been educated by people who tried to make us feel responsible for their feelings so we would feel guilty. Feelings are important, but we don't want to use them in that way. We don't want to use them in a guilt-inducing manner. It's very important that when we do express our feelings we follow our feelings with a statement that makes it clear that *the cause of our feelings is our needs.*

Q: What prevents people from just saying what they need?

A: Just as it's difficult for many people to develop a literacy of feelings, it's also very difficult for them to develop a literacy of needs. Many people in fact have very negative associations with needs. They associate needs with being needy, dependant, selfish, and again I think that comes from our history of educating people to fit well into domination structures so that they are obedient and submissive to authority. See, people do not make good slaves when they're in touch with their needs. I went to schools for twenty-one years, and I can't recall ever being asked what my needs were. And my education didn't focus on helping me be more alive, more in touch with myself and others. It was oriented toward rewarding me for getting right answers as defined by authorities. Look at the words that you are using to describe your needs. Needs do not contain any reference to specific people taking specific actions. Needs are universal. All human beings have the same needs.

When we can connect at the need level, when we see one another's humanness, it's amazing how conflicts which seem unsolvable become solvable. I do a lot of work with people in conflict. Husbands and wives, parents and children, tribes of people. Many of these people think they have a conflict which can't be resolved. And it's been amazing to me over the years that I've been doing conflict resolution and mediation work, what happens when you can get people over their diagnosis of one another, get them connected at the need level to what's going on in one another, how conflicts which seem impossible to resolve seem like they almost resolve themselves.

Q: *So what's next after feelings and needs?*

A: Now we have expressed the three pieces of information that are necessary to answer the question, "What's alive in us?" We've expressed what we're observing, what we're feeling, and the needs of ours that are connected to our feelings.

This brings us to the **second question**—and it's related to the first: "What can we do to make life more wonderful— what can you do to make life more wonderful for me; what can I do to make life more wonderful for you?" That's the other half of connecting with the Divine Energy in us: how to make empathic connection with what's alive in the other person in order to make life more wonderful for the other person. Let me tell you what I mean by empathic connection. Empathy, of course, is a special kind of understanding. It's not an understanding of the head where we just mentally understand what another person says. It's something far deeper and more precious than that. Empathic connection is an understanding of the heart where we see the beauty in the other person, the Divine Energy in the other person, the life that's alive in them. We connect with it. We don't mentally understand it, we connect with it. It doesn't mean we have to feel the same feelings as the other person. That's sympathy, when we feel sad, maybe that another person is upset. Now, it doesn't mean that we have to have the same feelings; it means that we are *with* the other person.

This quality of understanding requires one of the most precious gifts one human being can give to another: our presence in the moment. If we're mentally trying to understand the other person, we're not present with them in this moment. We're sitting there analyzing them, but we're not with them. So, empathic connection involves *connecting with what is alive in the other person at this moment.*

Q: *What keeps us from connecting to the life in each other as you suggest?*

A: We have been educated to think that there is something wrong with us. I want to suggest that you never, never, never hear what other people think about you. I predict you'll live longer, and you'll enjoy life more if you never hear what people think about you. Never take it personally. The recommendation I have is to learn to connect empathically with any message coming at us from other people. And Nonviolent Communication shows us a way of doing that. It shows us a way of seeing the beauty in the other person in any given moment, regardless of their behavior or their language. It requires connecting with the other person's feelings and needs at this moment, with what's alive in them. And when we do that, we're going to hear the other person singing a very beautiful song.

I was working with some twelve-year-olds in a school in the state of Washington, showing them how to make empathic connections with people. And they wanted me to show them how they could deal with parents and teachers. They were afraid what they would get back if they opened up and revealed what was alive in them. One of the students said: "Marshall, I was honest with one of my teachers. I said I didn't understand and I asked her to explain it again and the teacher said, 'Don't you listen? I've explained it twice already.'" Another young man said: "I asked my Dad yesterday for something. I tried to express my needs to him and he said, 'You're the most selfish child in the family.'" They were very eager to have me show them how to empathically connect with the people in their lives who use language like that. Because they only knew to take it personally, to think that there was something wrong with them. I showed the students that if you learn how to connect empathically with other people you will hear that they are always singing a beautiful song expressing their needs. That's what you will hear behind every message coming at you from another human being if you connect to the Divine Energy in that person at that moment.

Q: Can you give an example of how to make an empathic connection with someone?

A: We started by telling someone what they've done, how you feel, what needs of yours aren't getting met. Now, what can be done to make life more wonderful? This takes the form of a clear request. We need to request of the other person what we would like them to do to make life more wonderful for us. We've told them the pain we feel in relationship to what their behavior is, what needs of ours aren't getting met. Now we're going to say what we would like them to do to make life more wonderful for us.

Nonviolent Communication suggests that we make our request using positive action language. Let me explain what I mean. Positive in the sense of what you want the other person to do in contrast to what you don't want or what you want them to stop doing. We get to a different place with people when we are clear about what we want rather than just telling them what we don't want. A good example of that was a teacher recently in a workshop who said: "Oh, Marshall, you've just helped me understand what happened to me yesterday." I said, "What was that?" She said: "There was this boy tapping on his book while I was talking to the class. And I said, 'Would you please stop tapping on your book.' So, he started to tap on his desk."

You see, telling people what we don't want is far different than what we do want. When we try to get somebody to stop something, it makes punishment look like an effective strategy. But if we ask ourselves two questions, we would never use punishment again. We would never use it with children, we would create a judicial system, a correctional system, that does not punish criminals for what they've done and we wouldn't try to punish other nations for what they're doing to us. Punishment is a losing game. We would see that if we asked these two questions. Question number one: What do we want the other person to do? See, not what we don't want. *What do we want them to do?* Now, if we ask only that question, it can still make punishment seem like it works sometimes, because we can probably recall times when we've used punishment and we were successful at getting somebody to do what we wanted them to do. But, if we add a second question, punishment never works. And what is the second question? *What do we want the other person's reasons to be for doing what we want them to do?* The purpose of Nonviolent Communication is to create connections so people do things for one another out of compassion, out of connection to Divine Energy, to serve life. Not out of fear of punishment, not out of hope for rewards, but because of the natural joy we feel of contributing to one another's well-being. So, when we make our request we want to do it in the positive, what we do want.

Q: How do you express your needs as requests without sounding like you're demanding something?

A: We do want to make clear assertive requests, but we want other people to know that these are requests and not demands. Now, what's the difference? First, you can't tell the difference by how nicely it is asked. So, if we do say to someone living with us, "I would like you to hang up your clothes when you're finished with them," is that a request or a demand? We don't know yet. You can never tell whether something is a request or a demand by how nicely it is asked or how clear it is. What determines the difference between a request and a demand is how we treat people when they don't do as we've asked. That's what tells people whether we make requests or demands.

Now, what happens when people hear demands? Well, it's pretty obvious with some people when they've heard your request as a demand. One time I asked my youngest son, "Would you please hang your coat up in the closet?" And he said, "Who was your slave before I was born?" OK, well, it's easy to be around such a person because if they hear your request as a demand you know it right away. But other people when they hear a request as a demand respond quite differently. They'll say, "OK," but then they don't do it. Or the worst case is when the person hears the demand and they say, "OK," and they do it. But they did it because they heard a demand. They were afraid of what would happen to them if they didn't. Anytime somebody does what we ask out of guilt, shame, duty, obligation, fear of punishment, anything that people do for us out of that energy, we're going to pay for it. We want people to do for us only when they're connected to that kind of a Divine Energy that exists in all of us. Divine Energy is manifest to me by the joy we feel in giving to one another. We're not doing it to avoid punishment, guilt, and all of those things.

Q: What about discipline? What you're suggesting sounds like just being permissive.

A: Some people cannot believe that you can have order in the house and the government unless you force people to do things, unless you make demands. For example, one mother I was working with said: "But, Marshall, that's all very well and good, to hope that people are going to respond out of Divine Energy, but what about a child? I mean, a child has to first learn what they *have to* do, what they *should* do." This mother was using two of the words, or concepts, that I think are the most destructive concepts on the planet today: *have to* and *should*. She didn't trust that there's Divine Energy in children as well as in adults so that they can do things not because they're going to be punished if they don't, but because they see the joy that comes from contributing to other people's well-being.

I said to the mother: "I hope today I can show you other ways of presenting things to your children so that it's more of a request. They see your needs. They don't do it because they think they have to. They see the choice and they respond out of this Divine Energy within themselves." She says, "I do all kinds of things every day that I hate to do, but there are just some things you *have to* do." I said, "Could you give me an example?" She said: "OK. Here's one. When I leave here this evening, I have to go home and cook. I hate to cook. I hate it with a passion, but it's just one of those things you have to do. I've done it every day for twenty years. I hate it, but you have to do certain things." See, she wasn't cooking out of Divine Energy. She was doing that out of this other kind of consciousness. So, I said to her: "Well, I'm hoping I can show you today a way of thinking and communicating that will help you get back in touch with your Divine Energy and make sure that you only come out of that. And you can then present things to others so that they can come out of that energy."

She was a rapid learner. She went home that very night and announced to her family that she no longer wanted to cook. And I got some feedback from her family. About three weeks later, who shows up at a training but her two older sons. They came up before the training and said to me, "We want to tell you how much change has occurred in our family since our mother came to your workshop." I said: "Oh, yeah. You know, I've been very curious. She told me all the changes she's been making in her life, and I'm always wondering how that affects other family members. So, I'm glad you guys showed up tonight. For example, what was it like that first night when she came home and said she no longer wanted to cook?" The oldest son said to me: "Marshall, I said to myself, 'Thank God. Now maybe she won't complain after every meal.'"

Q: *How can I tell when I'm connecting to what's alive in someone else?*

A: When we do things that don't come out of this Divine Energy in each of us, this Divine Energy that makes compassionate giving natural, when we come out of any culturally learned pattern of doing things because we should, have to, must, out of guilt, out of shame, duty, obligation, or to get rewards, *everybody* pays for it, everybody. Nonviolent Communication wants us to be clear, to not respond unless our response is coming out of this Divine Energy. And you'll know it is when you are willing to do what is requested. Even if it's hard work, it will be joyful if your only motive is to make life more wonderful.

Now, when we put this all together then, it looks like this: We may start a dialogue with the other person by telling them what's alive in us and what we would like them to do to make life more wonderful for us. Then no matter how they respond, we try to connect with what's alive in them and what would make life more wonderful for them. And we keep this flow of communication going until we find strategies to meet everybody's needs, and we want to always be sure that whatever strategies people agree to, they're agreeing freely out of a willing desire to contribute to the well-being of one another.

Q: *Can you give another example of how you've actually used this process to connect with others?*

I was working in a refugee camp in a country not very pleased with the United States. And when my interpreter announced that I was an American citizen, there were about a hundred and seventy people assembled, and one of them jumped up and screamed at me, "Murderer." I was glad I knew Nonviolent Communication that day. It enabled me to see the beauty behind that person's message, what was alive and human in him. And we do that in Nonviolent Communication by hearing feelings and needs behind any message. So I said to this gentleman, "Are you feeling angry because your need for support isn't getting met by my country?" Now, that required me to try to sense what he was feeling and needing. I could have been wrong. But even if we're wrong, if we are sincerely trying to connect with the Divine Energy in another human being—their feelings, their needs at that moment—that shows the other person that no matter how they communicate with us, we care about what's alive in them, and when a person trusts that, we're well on our way to making a connection that everybody's needs can get met. But, it didn't happen right away because this gentleman was in a lot of pain.

And it happened that I guessed right, because when I said, "Are you angry because your need for support isn't being met by my country?" he said, "You're darn right," and he added to that: "We don't have sewage systems. We don't have housing. Why are you sending your weapons?" So, I said, "So, sir, if I'm hearing you again you're saying that it's very painful when you need things like sewage systems and you need things like housing and when weapons are sent instead it's very painful." He said: "Of course. Do you know what it's like to live under these conditions for twenty-eight years?" "So, sir, you're saying that it's very painful and you need some understanding for the conditions that you're living under." An hour later, the gentleman invited me to a Ramadan dinner at his house.

This is what happens when we can connect with what's alive in us, the humanness in one another, the feelings and needs behind any message. This doesn't mean that we always have to say it out loud. Sometimes it's pretty obvious what the person is feeling and needing; we don't have to say it. They'll feel it from our eyes whether we are really trying to connect with them. Notice this does not require that we agree with the other person. It doesn't mean we have to like what they're saying. It means that we give them this precious gift of our presence, to be present at this moment to what's alive in this person and that we are interested in that, sincerely interested. Not as a psychological technique, but because we want to connect with the Divine Energy in that person at this moment.

Q: The process of connecting to the Divine Energy in others with NVC seems clear enough on paper, but isn't it hard to actually live by?

Just about everybody that studies Nonviolent Communication says two things about it. First they say how easy it is; I mean, how simple. Just the two questions, and all we have to do is keep our communication, our focus of attention, our consciousness, on what's alive in us and on what would make life more wonderful. How simple. The second thing they say about it is how difficult it is. Now, how can something be so simple and so difficult at the same time?

It's difficult because we haven't been taught to think about what's alive in us. We have been educated to fit under structures in which a few people dominate many. We have been taught to pay the most attention to what people—especially the authorities—think of us. We know that if they judge us as bad, wrong, incompetent, stupid, lazy, selfish, we're going to get punished. And if they label us as good or bad little boys and girls, good or bad employees, then we could be rewarded or punished. So, we haven't been educated to think in terms of what's alive in us and what would make life more wonderful. Nonviolent Communication suggests that we let people know what's alive in us in relationship to what they're doing. We want to be honest in Nonviolent Communication, but we want to be honest without using any words that imply enemy images, wrongness, criticism, insults, and psychological diagnosis.

Many people believe that you just can't do this with some people. They believe that some people are so damaged, so whatever, that no matter what communication you use, you're not going to arrive at this point. That has not been my experience. It just might take some time. Like when I'm working in one of the various prisons throughout the world, I'm not saying that this connection can happen right away. It may take quite awhile for someone being punished for a crime to really trust that I'm sincerely interested in what's alive in them. Sometimes it's not easy to stay with that because my own cultural conditioning hasn't allowed me to be fluent at this earlier in my life, so learning this can be a real challenge.

Q: *How do you get enemies to recognize the Divine in each other?*

A: When you get people connected at the level of Divine Energy it's hard to maintain those "enemy" images. Nonviolent Communication in its purity is the most powerful, quickest way I've found to get people to go from life-alienated ways of thinking where they want to hurt each other, to enjoying giving to each other.

When I have had a couple of people facing each other, Hutu and Tutsi, and their families have been killed by each other, it's amazing that in two or three hours, we can get them nurturing each other. It's inevitable. *Inevitable.* That's why I use this approach.

Given the amount of suffering that has gone on it amazes me how simple it is, and how quickly it can happen. Nonviolent Communication really quickly heals people who have experienced a lot of pain. This motivates me to want to make it happen even more quickly because the way we're doing it now with just a few people at a time still takes a while.

How do we get this done more quickly with the other eight hundred thousand Hutus and Tutsis that didn't come to our training, and the rest of the planet? I would like to explore what would happen if we could make movies or television shows of this process, because I've seen that when two people go through the process with other people watching, that vicarious learning, healing, and reconciliations happen. I would like to explore ways to use the media to get masses of people to go quickly through this process together.

Q: How basic is our need to give to one another?

A: I think the need to enrich life is one of the most basic and powerful needs we all have. Now another way to say this is that we need to act from the Divine Energy within us. And I think that when we "are" that Divine Energy that there is nothing we like more—nothing in which we find more joy—than enriching life, than using our immense power to enrich life.

But whenever we are trying to meet this need of ours to "live" this Divine Energy, trying to contribute to life, there is also another need, and a request that goes with it. We have a need for information and so we make a request for feedback from the person whose life we are trying to enrich. We want to know, "Is my intention being fulfilled by my action; was my attempt to contribute successful?"

In our culture that request gets distorted into our thinking that we have a "need" for the other person to love us for what we've done, to appreciate what we've done, to approve of us for what we've done. And that distorts and screws up the beauty of the whole process. It wasn't their approval that we needed. Our very intent was to use our energy to enrich life. But we need the feedback. How do I know my effort was successful unless I get feedback?

And I can use this feedback to help me know if I am coming out of Divine Energy. I know that I am coming out of Divine Energy when I am able to value a criticism as much as a thank you.

Q: *Have you encountered any cultural or language barriers to this process?*

A: It amazes me how few and how little they are. When I first started to teach this process in another language I really doubted that it could be done. I remember the first time I was in Europe I was going to go first to Munich and then to Geneva. My colleague and I both doubted that we could get this through in another language. She was going to do it in French, and I would be there for her to ask me questions if something came up. I was going to at least try to see if we could go through translators. But it worked so well without any problems, and I find the same thing everywhere. So I just don't worry about it, I'll do it in English, and you translate it and it works very well. I can't think of any culture that we've had any problem with other than little things, but not with the essence of it. Not only have we had no problem but also repeatedly, after trainings all over the world, there are variations of people telling me that this is essentially what their religion says. It's old stuff, they know this stuff, and they're grateful for this manifestation, but it's nothing new.

Q: Do you believe a spiritual practice is important for practicing nonviolence?

A: I recommend in all workshops that people take time to ask themselves this question, "How do I choose to connect with other human beings?" and to be as conscious as they can about that. To make sure it's their choice and not the way they've been programmed to choose. Really, what is the way you would choose to connect with other human beings?

Gratitude also plays a big role for me. If I am conscious of a human act that I want to express gratitude for, conscious of how I feel when the act occurs, whether it's my act or someone else's, and what needs of mine it fulfills, then expressing gratitude fills me with consciousness of the power that we human beings have to enrich lives. It makes me aware that we are Divine Energy, that we have such power to make life wonderful, and that there is nothing we like better than to do just that.

To me, that is powerful evidence of our Divine Energy, that we have this power to make life so wonderful, and that there is nothing we like more. That's why part of my spiritual practice is to be conscious of gratitude and expressing gratitude.

Q: Have you been influenced by past movements that have attempted to mediate between spirituality and social change, like Gandhi's or Martin Luther King Jr.'s?

A: Well, I certainly have been affected by them, because I've studied people historically that were getting things done in a way that I value and they certainly are two people that were doing that. The kind of spirituality I value is one in which you get great joy out of contributing to life, not just sitting and meditating, although meditation is certainly valuable. But, from the meditation, from the resulting consciousness, I would like to see people in action creating the world that they want to live in.

Recommended Reading:

Spirit Matters by Michael Lerner

A Spirituality of Resistance by Roger S. Gottlieb

Open and Closed Mind by Milton Rokeach

The Powers That Be by Walter Wink

The Four-Part Nonviolent Communication Process

Clearly expressing how **I am** without blaming or criticizing	Empathically receiving how **you are** without hearing blame or criticism

OBSERVATIONS

1. What I observe *(see, hear, remember, imagine, free from my evaluations)* that does or does not contribute to my well-being:

   "When I (see, hear) . . . "

1. What you observe *(see, hear, remember, imagine, free from your evaluations)* that does or does not contribute to your well-being:

   "When you see/hear . . . "

   (Sometimes unspoken when offering empathy)

FEELINGS

2. How I feel *(emotion or sensation rather than thought)* in relation to what I observe:

   "I feel . . . "

2. How you feel *(emotion or sensation rather than thought)* in relation to what you observe:

   "You feel . . ."

NEEDS

3. What I need or value *(rather than a preference, or a specific action)* that causes my feelings:

   " . . . because I need/value . . . "

3. What you need or value *(rather than a preference, or a specific action)* that causes your feelings:

   " . . . because you need/value . . ."

Clearly requesting that which would enrich **my** life without demanding	Empathically receiving that which would enrich **your** life without hearing any demand

REQUESTS

4. The concrete actions I would like taken:

   "Would you be willing to . . . ?"

4. The concrete actions you would like taken:

   "Would you like . . . ?"

   (Sometimes unspoken when offering empathy)

Some Basic Feelings We All Have

Feelings when needs are fulfilled

- Amazed
- Comfortable
- Confident
- Eager
- Energetic
- Fulfilled
- Glad
- Hopeful
- Inspired
- Intrigued
- Joyous
- Moved
- Optimistic
- Proud
- Relieved
- Stimulated
- Surprised
- Thankful
- Touched
- Trustful

Feelings when needs are not fulfilled

- Angry
- Annoyed
- Concerned
- Confused
- Disappointed
- Discouraged
- Distressed
- Embarrassed
- Frustrated
- Helpless
- Hopeless
- Impatient
- Irritated
- Lonely
- Nervous
- Overwhelmed
- Puzzled
- Reluctant
- Sad
- Uncomfortable

Some Basic Needs We All Have

Autonomy
- Choosing dreams/goals/values
- Choosing plans for fulfilling one's dreams, goals, values

Celebration
- Celebrating the creation of life and dreams fulfilled
- Celebrating losses: loved ones, dreams, etc. (mourning)

Integrity
- Authenticity • Creativity
- Meaning • Self-worth

Interdependence
- Acceptance • Appreciation
- Closeness • Community
- Consideration
- Contribution to the enrichment of life
- Emotional Safety • Empathy

Physical Nurturance
- Air • Food
- Movement, exercise
- Protection from life-threatening forms of life: viruses, bacteria, insects, predatory animals
- Rest • Sexual Expression
- Shelter • Touch • Water

Play
- Fun • Laughter

Spiritual Communion
- Beauty • Harmony
- Inspiration • Order • Peace

- Honesty (the empowering honesty that enables us to learn from our limitations)
- Love • Reassurance
- Respect • Support
- Trust • Understanding

About PuddleDancer Press

PuddleDancer Press (PDP) is the main publisher of Nonviolent Communication™ related works. Its mission is to provide high-quality materials to help people create a world in which all needs are met compassionately. By working in partnership with the Center for Nonviolent Communication and NVC trainers, teams, and local supporters, PDP has created a comprehensive promotion effort that has helped bring NVC to thousands of new people each year.

Since 1998 PDP has donated more than 60,000 NVC books to organizations, decision-makers, and individuals in need around the world.

Visit the PDP website at www.NonviolentCommunication.com to find the following resources:

- **Shop NVC**—Continue your learning. Purchase our NVC titles online safely, affordably, and conveniently. Find everyday discounts on individual titles, multiple-copies, and book packages. Learn more about our authors and read endorsements of NVC from world-renowned communication experts and peacemakers. www.NonviolentCommunication.com/store/

- **NVC Quick Connect e-Newsletter**—Sign up today to receive our monthly e-Newsletter, filled with expert articles, upcoming training opportunities with our authors, and exclusive specials on NVC learning materials. Archived e-Newsletters are also available

- **About NVC**—Learn more about these life-changing communication and conflict resolution skills including an overview of the NVC process, key facts about NVC, and more.

- **About Marshall Rosenberg**—Access press materials, biography, and more about this world-renowned peacemaker, educator, bestselling author, and founder of the Center for Nonviolent Communication.

- **Free Resources for Learning NVC**—Find free weekly tips series, NVC article archive, and other great resources to make learning these vital communication skills just a little easier.

For more information, please contact PuddleDancer Press at:

2240 Encinitas Blvd., Ste. D-911 • Encinitas, CA 92024
Phone: 760-652-5754 • Fax: 760-274-6400
Email: email@puddledancer.com • www.NonviolentCommunication.com

About the Center for Nonviolent Communication

The Center for Nonviolent Communication (CNVC) is an international nonprofit peacemaking organization whose vision is a world where everyone's needs are met peacefully. CNVC is devoted to supporting the spread of Nonviolent Communication (NVC) around the world.

Founded in 1984 by Dr. Marshall B. Rosenberg, CNVC has been contributing to a vast social transformation in thinking, speaking and acting—showing people how to connect in ways that inspire compassionate results. NVC is now being taught around the globe in communities, schools, prisons, mediation centers, churches, businesses, professional conferences, and more. Hundreds of certified trainers and hundreds more supporters teach NVC to tens of thousands of people each year in more than 60 countries.

CNVC believes that NVC training is a crucial step to continue building a compassionate, peaceful society. Your tax-deductible donation will help CNVC continue to provide training in some of the most impoverished, violent corners of the world. It will also support the development and continuation of organized projects aimed at bringing NVC training to high-need geographic regions and populations.

To make a tax-deductible donation or to learn more about the valuable resources described below, visit the CNVC website at www.CNVC.org:

- **Training and Certification**—Find local, national, and international training opportunities, access trainer certification information, connect to local NVC communities, trainers, and more.

- **CNVC Bookstore**—Find mail or phone order information for a complete selection of NVC books, booklets, audio, and video materials at the CNVC website.

- **CNVC Projects**—Participate in one of the several regional and theme-based projects that provide focus and leadership for teaching NVC in a particular application or geographic region.

- **E-Groups and List Servs**—Join one of several moderated, topic-based NVC e-groups and list servs developed to support individual learning and the continued growth of NVC worldwide.

For more information, please contact CNVC at:

9301 Indian School Rd., NE, Suite 204, Albuquerque, NM 87112-2861
Ph: 505-244-4041 • US Only: 800-255-7696 • Fax: 505-247-0414
Email: cnvc@CNVC.org • Website: www.CNVC.org

Speak Peace in a World of Conflict
What You Say Next Will Change Your World
By Marshall B. Rosenberg, PhD

$15.95 — Trade Paper 5-3/8x8-3/8, 208pp
ISBN: 978-1-892005-17-5

International peacemaker, mediator, and healer, Marshall Rosenberg shows you how the language you use is the key to enriching life. *Speak Peace* is filled with inspiring stories, lessons, and ideas drawn from more than forty years of mediating conflicts and healing relationships in some of the most war-torn, impoverished, and violent corners of the world. Find insight, practical skills, and powerful tools that will profoundly change your relationships and the course of your life for the better.

Discover how you can create an internal consciousness of peace as the first step toward effective personal, professional, and social change. Find complete chapters on the mechanics of Speaking Peace, conflict resolution, transforming business culture, transforming enemy images, addressing terrorism, transforming authoritarian structures, expressing and receiving gratitude, and social change.

Peaceful Living
Daily Meditations for Living With Love, Healing, and Compassion
By Mary Mackenzie

$19.95 — Trade Paper 5x7.5, 448pp
ISBN: 978-1-892005-19-9

In this gathering of wisdom, Mary Mackenzie empowers you with an intimate life map that will literally change the course of your life for the better. Each of the 366 meditations includes an inspirational quote and concrete, practical tips for integrating the daily message into your life. The learned behaviors of cynicism, resentment, and getting even are replaced with the skills of Nonviolent Communication, including recognizing one's needs and values and making choices in alignment with them.

Peaceful Living goes beyond daily affirmations, providing the skills and consciousness you need to transform relationships, heal pain, and discover the life-enriching meaning behind even the most trying situations. Begin each day centered and connected to yourself and your values. Direct the course of your life toward your deepest hopes and needs. Ground yourself in the power of compassionate, conscious living.

Available from PuddleDancer Press, the Center for Nonviolent Communication, all major bookstores, and Amazon.com. Distributed by Independent Publisher's Group: 800-888-4741.

Nonviolent Communication:
A Language of Life, 3rd Edition
Life-Changing Tools for Healthy Relationships
By Marshall B. Rosenberg, PhD

$19.95 — Trade Paper 6x9, 264pp
ISBN: 978-1-892005-28-1

What is "Violent" Communication?

If "violent" means acting in ways that result in hurt or harm, then much of how we communicate—judging others, bullying, having racial bias, blaming, finger pointing, discriminating, speaking without listening, criticizing others or ourselves, name-calling, reacting when angry, using political rhetoric, being defensive or judging who's "good/bad" or what's "right/wrong" with people—could indeed be called "violent communication."

What is "Nonviolent" Communication?

Nonviolent Communication is the integration of 4 things:

Consciousness: a set of principles that support living a life of compassion, collaboration, courage, and authenticity

Language: understanding how words contribute to connection or distance

Communication: knowing how to ask for what we want, how to hear others even in disagreement, and how to move toward solutions that work for all

Means of influence: sharing "power with others" rather than using "power over others"

SAVE an extra 10% at NonviolentCommunication.com with code: **bookads**

Nonviolent Communication
Companion Workbook, 2nd Edition
A Practical Guide for Individual, Group, or Classroom Study
By Lucy Leu

$21.95 — Trade Paper 7x10, 240pp
ISBN: 978-1-892005-29-8

Learning Nonviolent Communication has often been equated with learning a whole new language. The *NVC Companion Workbook* helps you put these powerful, effective skills into practice with chapter-by-chapter study of Marshall Rosenberg's cornerstone text, *NVC: A Language of Life*. Create a safe, supportive group learning or practice environment that nurtures the needs of each participant. Find a wealth of activities, exercises, and facilitator suggestions to refine and practice this powerful communication process.

Nonviolent Communication has flourished for more than four decades across sixty countries selling more than 1,000,000 books for a simple reason: it works.

Available from PuddleDancer Press, the Center for Nonviolent Communication, all major bookstores, and Amazon.com. Distributed by Independent Publisher's Group: 800-888-4741.

Being Genuine

Stop Being Nice, Start Being Real

By Thomas d'Ansembourg

$17.95 — Trade Paper 5-3/8x8-3/8, 280pp
ISBN: 978-1-892005-21-2

Being Genuine brings Thomas d'Ansembourg's blockbuster French title to the English market. His work offers you a fresh new perspective on the proven skills offered in the bestselling book, *Nonviolent Communication: A Language of Life*. Drawing on his own real-life examples and stories, Thomas d'Ansembourg provides practical skills and concrete steps that allow us to safely remove the masks we wear, which prevent the intimacy and satisfaction we desire with our intimate partners, children, parents, friends, family, and colleagues.

"Through this book, we can feel Nonviolent Communication not as a formula but as a rich, meaningful way of life, both intellectually and emotionally."

—**Vicki Robin,** co-founder, Conversation Cafes, coauthor, *Your Money or Your Life*

Based on Marshall Rosenberg's Nonviolent Communication process

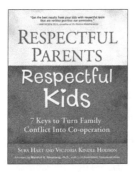

Respectful Parents, Respectful Kids

7 Keys to Turn Family Conflict Into Co-operation

By Sura Hart and Victoria Kindle Hodson

$17.95 — Trade Paper 7.5x9.25, 256pp
ISBN: 978-1-892005-22-9

Stop the Struggle—Find the Co-operation and Mutual Respect You Want!

Do more than simply correct bad behavior—finally unlock your parenting potential. Use this handbook to move beyond typical discipline techniques and begin creating an environment based on mutual respect, emotional safety, and positive, open communication. *Respectful Parents, Respectful Kids* offers *7 Simple Keys* to discover the mutual respect and nurturing relationships you've been looking for.

Use these 7 Keys to:

- Set firm limits without using demands or coercion
- Achieve mutual respect without being submissive
- Successfully prevent, reduce, and resolve conflicts
- Empower your kids to open up, co-operate, and realize their full potential
- Make your home a *No-Fault Zone* where trust thrives

Available from PuddleDancer Press, the Center for Nonviolent Communication, all major bookstores, and Amazon.com. Distributed by Independent Publisher's Group: 800-888-4741.

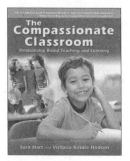

The Compassionate Classroom

Relationship Based Teaching and Learning

By Sura Hart and Victoria Kindle Hodson

$17.95 — Trade Paper 7.5x9.25, 208pp
ISBN: 978-1-892005-06-9

When Compassion Thrives, So Does Learning

Learn powerful skills to create an emotionally safe learning environment where academic excellence thrives. Build trust, reduce conflict, improve co-operation, and maximize the potential of each student as you create relationship-centered classrooms. This how-to guide offers customizable exercises, activities, charts, and cutouts that make it easy for educators to create lesson plans for a day, a week, or an entire school year. An exceptional resource for educators, homeschool parents, child-care providers, and mentors.

"Education is not simply about teachers covering a curriculum; it is a dance of relationships. *The Compassionate Classroom* presents both the case for teaching compassionately and a wide range of practical tools to maximize student potential."

—Tim Seldin, president, The Montessori Foundation

The No-Fault Classroom

Tools to Resolve Conflict & Foster Relationship Intelligence

By Sura Hart and Victoria Kindle Hodson

$17.95 — Trade Paper 8.5x11, 256pp
ISBN: 978-1-892005-18-2

Students Can Resolve Their Own Conflicts!

Offering far more than discipline techniques that move aggressive behavior out of the classroom to the playground or sidewalk, *The No-Fault Classroom* leads students ages 7–12 to develop skills in problem solving, empathic listening, and conflict resolution that will last a lifetime.

The book's 21 interactive and step-by-step lessons, construction materials, and adaptable scripts give educators the tools they need to return order and co-operation to the classroom and jumpstart engaged learning—from the rural school to the inner city, the charter school, to the home school classroom. *Curricular Tie-ins* guide teachers to use the conflict resolution tools they've developed to meet state learning requirements in social studies, language arts, history, reading, and science.

Available from PuddleDancer Press, the Center for Nonviolent Communication, all major bookstores, and Amazon.com. Distributed by Independent Publisher's Group: 800-888-4741.

Being Me, Loving You: *A Practical Guide to Extraordinary Relationships* **by Marshall B. Rosenberg, PhD** • Watch your relationships strengthen as you learn to think of love as something you "do," something you give freely from the heart.
80pp, ISBN: 978-1-892005-16-8 • **$6.95**

Getting Past the Pain Between Us: *Healing and Reconciliation Without Compromise* **by Marshall B. Rosenberg, PhD** • Learn simple steps to create the heartfelt presence necessary for lasting healing to occur—great for mediators, counselors, families, and couples.
48pp, ISBN: 978-1-892005-07-6 • **$6.95**

Graduating From Guilt: *Six Steps to Overcome Guilt and Reclaim Your Life* **by Holly Michelle Eckert** • The burden of guilt leaves us stuck, stressed, and feeling like we can never measure up. Through a proven six-step process, this book helps liberate you from the toxic guilt, blame, and shame you carry.
96pp, ISBN: 978-1-892005-23-6 • **$9.95**

The Heart of Social Change: *How to Make a Difference in Your World* **by Marshall B. Rosenberg, PhD** • Learn how creating an internal consciousness of compassion can impact your social change efforts.
48pp, ISBN: 978-1-892005-10-6 • **$6.95**

Humanizing Health Care: *Creating Cultures of Compassion With Nonviolent Communication* **by Melanie Sears, RN, MBA, PhD** • Leveraging more than twenty-five years nursing experience, Melanie demonstrates the profound effectiveness of NVC to create lasting, positive improvements to patient care and the health care workplace.
112pp, ISBN: 978-1-892005-26-7 • **$7.95**

Parenting From Your Heart: *Sharing the Gifts of Compassion, Connection, and Choice* **by Inbal Kashtan** • Filled with insight and practical skills, this booklet will help you transform your parenting to address every day challenges.
48pp, ISBN: 978-1-892005-08-3 • **$6.95**

Photo by Beth Banning

Marshall B. Rosenberg, PhD (1934–2015) founded and was for many years the Director of Educational Services for the Center for Nonviolent Communication, an international peacemaking organization.

During his life he authored fifteen books, including the bestselling *Nonviolent Communication: A Language of Life* (PuddleDancer Press), which has sold more than one million copies worldwide and has been translated into more than 30 languages, with more translations in the works.

Dr. Rosenberg has received a number of awards for his Nonviolent Communication work including:

2014: Champion of Forgiveness Award from the Worldwide Forgiveness Alliance
2006: Bridge of Peace Nonviolence Award from the Global Village Foundation
2005: Light of God Expressing in Society Award from the Association of Unity Churches
2004: Religious Science International Golden Works Award
2004: International Peace Prayer Day Man of Peace Award by the Healthy, Happy Holy (3HO) Organization
2002: Princess Anne of England and Chief of Police Restorative Justice Appreciation Award
2000: International Listening Association Listener of the Year Award

Dr. Rosenberg first used the NVC process in federally funded school integration projects to provide mediation and communication skills training during the 1960s. The Center for Nonviolent Communication, which he founded in 1984, now has hundreds of certified NVC trainers and supporters teaching NVC in more than sixty countries around the globe.

A sought-after presenter, peacemaker and visionary leader, Dr. Rosenberg led NVC workshops and international intensive trainings for tens of thousands of people in over 60 countries across the world and provided training and initiated peace programs in many war-torn areas including Nigeria, Sierra Leone, and the Middle East. He worked tirelessly with educators, managers, health care providers, lawyers, military officers, prisoners, police and prison officials, government officials, and individual families. With guitar and puppets in hand and a spiritual energy that filled a room, Marshall showed us how to create a more peaceful and satisfying world.